SCIENCE AND SOCIETY™

CHEMICAL AND BIOLOGICAL WEAPONS

AGENTS OF WAR AND TERROR

Daniel E. Harmon

ROSEN
PUBLISHING®

New York

Published in 2009 by The Rosen Publishing Group, Inc.
29 East 21st Street, New York, NY 10010

Copyright © 2009 by The Rosen Publishing Group, Inc.

First Edition

Library of Congress Cataloging-in-Publication Data

Harmon, Daniel E.
Chemical and biological weapons : agents of war and terror / Daniel E. Harmon.
     p. cm.—(Science and society)
Includes bibliographical references and index.
ISBN-13: 978-1-4358-5023-1 (library binding)
1. Chemical warfare—Juvenile literature. 2. Biological warfare—Juvenile literature. I. Title.
UG447.H365 2009
358.3—dc22

                                                                        2008013417

Manufactured in Malaysia

On the cover: A member of the U.S. Marine Corps Chemical/Biological Incident Response Force prepares to enter a building to sweep for anthrax.

CONTENTS

Most forms of science are used for human good. Sometimes, though, science is used for evil. This is a story of bad science—the science of terror.

The spread of harmful chemicals and biological organisms can injure and kill thousands of people and make an infected area unlivable for some time to come. Such events actually have occurred. When they do, they usually result from careless pollution or natural causes. But scientists also know how to spread them deliberately. Biochemical substances can become horrifying weapons.

In the age of modern terrorism, many people fear militant organizations will unleash chemical and biological weapons (CBWs) in public places such as mass transit systems, sports arenas, and schools. Different scenarios have been suggested by authors of popular fiction and makers of thriller films, and other schemes trouble the imagination. Killer bacteria spread through the air-conditioning system of a public building. Terrorists in a van cruise along a thoroughfare upwind of a packed football stadium, spraying anthrax into the air. A bomb explodes in a crowded village square, causing more than physical demolition, for it contains deadly chemicals. Terrorists secretly place bags of poison liquid in subway trains, puncture them, and inconspicuously exit as fumes begin to spread through the cars. This last plot was carried out in Japan in 1995.

Experts observe, though, that up to this point in history, known incidents of biochemical attacks have been rare. When they have occurred, they are usually the work of an angry or psychologically disturbed individual, an assassin, or a blackmailer, not an organization. Fears persist, though, because numerous terrorist groups are known to possess such weapons. On a larger scale, the governments of many nations have developed and stockpiled them. They were widely used during World War I (1914–1918).

The malicious use of chemicals and plagues has taken many forms throughout history. Since ancient times, murderers have used poisons as lethal weapons. Ill-fated leaders have used them to commit suicide. Infamous examples include Queen Cleopatra of Egypt, who, according to lore, allowed herself to be bitten by a deadly serpent. Ancient armies

Subway passengers in Japan await medical aid after breathing sarin, a nerve gas released by terrorists in 1995. Twelve victims died; more than three thousand were sickened.

were known to poison wells and leave contaminated food for their enemies to capture. They tried to infest opposing forces and cities with plague-bearing rodents and insects.

People today like to believe that modern society is much more civilized. Even in war, it would be nice to know that all the world's armies play by certain rules, that certain kinds of horrors will never be inflicted. Events since the 1980s, however, have shown that not everyone abides by treaties or refrains from using banned weapons such as harmful chemicals and disease-causing organisms.

Alarmists warn that chemical and biological terrorism threatens great numbers of people (including children, medical patients, and civilian populations in general). Theoretically, terrorists can devastate crops and poison waters. Worse, they can create panic that paralyzes an entire populace and affects the economy of the civilized world. Even if it causes little actual damage, any reported chemical or biological attack can plunge society into hopelessness and shock. The anthrax mailings in the United States in 2001 was a real-life example of the psychology of terrorism.

What are these weapons? Who uses them, and why? And how much of a threat are they to our way of life?

Chapter One

WHAT ARE CHEMICAL AND BIOLOGICAL WEAPONS?

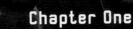

C hemical weapons are various types of devices that have as their payload or warhead a poisonous chemical agent. Some substances developed to be used as weapons are compounds or binary chemicals—items that are not harmful individually but can be deadly if combined.

Biological weapons employ tiny living life forms, or microorganisms, to spread sickness. Microorganisms that can cause diseases are called pathogens. Dangerous biological agents include viruses, bacteria, fungi, and parasites. New strains of hazardous germs come to light from time to time. It is also possible for terrorists and military biologists to deploy organisms that can cause age-old diseases. These could include pneumococci

Tuberculosis (TB) patients in Cambodia are among millions who have gotten the disease in recent years. At one time, medical scientists believed TB had been conquered, but new strains of it have taken many lives.

(Streptococcus pneumoniae), which produce bacterial pneumonia, and *Mycobacterium tuberculosis*, an organism that causes highly contagious tuberculosis (TB). Although scientists believed they had conquered such diseases years ago, these and other illnesses can return in altered forms. The World Health Organization declared TB to be a global emergency in 1993. During the 1990s, it killed as many as three million people per year worldwide. Despite continuing efforts to stop it, the disease still accounts for one-and-a-half million to two million deaths each year.

Chemical and biological weapons as a whole are abbreviated CBWs. Like nuclear weapons, they are considered weapons of

What Are Weapons of Mass Destruction?

WMDs are unconventional devices of warfare. The ultimate weapon of mass destruction is the nuclear missile, which can obliterate a large target from a distance. On a smaller scale, terrorists are developing WMDs to accomplish political goals that they cannot accomplish by military might.

Terrorists are interested in these weapons not simply to eliminate or neutralize opposing armed forces but potentially to wreak havoc on large civilian populations. Why? Because by doing so, they believe they can force not only an opposing army but an entire nation to give in to their demands. Terrorist leaders know they cannot overpower their adversaries' armed forces, but they can panic the civilian population of the opposing state or nation. In doing so, they can apply political pressure on the enemy government. Terrorist acts are believed to have affected the outcomes of elections.

Most modern nations, recognizing the horrible effects WMDs can have on civilian populations, have banned their use.

mass destruction (WMDs) because they potentially can harm or kill thousands, possibly *millions*, of people.

For chemical and biological agents to be used as weapons, effective delivery systems are required. In most past cases, they have been disseminated into the air by rockets or sprayed from airplanes. Obviously, weather conditions, especially wind changes, make them unpredictable.

They can also enter the food supply. More subtle distribution methods make them especially frightening. In the anthrax scare of 2001 in the United States, anthrax powder was mailed in letters from an anonymous sender or senders.

These types of agents attack the human body in different ways. They can be harmful or lethal if inhaled or consumed in food and water. Other forms can be fatal if they simply touch the skin, because skin pores naturally absorb them into the body.

Types of Chemical Weapons

There are a variety of chemical weapons. The following are the most common types with their known effects:

- Nerve chemicals destroy the nervous system. They attack an enzyme called acetylcholinesterase and prevent it from coordinating the nervous system. Inhalation or a miniscule touch of certain nerve agents on the skin can shut down the body and cause death in minutes. Nerve agents include VX, sarin, soman, and tabun.
- Choking chemicals attack the respiratory system. Examples are chlorine and phosgene. Chlorine destroys the lining of the respiratory tract. Phosgene causes water in the lungs— a pneumonia-like effect.
- Blood chemicals enter the bloodstream and prevent it from delivering oxygen to vital organs. This condition of insufficient oxygen in the blood is called anoxia. Hydrogen cyanide is the most common agent of this type.
- Blister chemicals damage the skin, eyes, and internal surfaces, including the lungs. Mustard gas, used repeatedly during World War I, is the most notorious example. Another common example is tear gas, which burns the skin and irritates the eyes. Some forms of tear gas cause choking and vomiting. Tear gas is often used by police and army units for riot control and for forcing fugitives from concealed places.

Chemical agents have been used to destroy plant life as well as human life. During the Vietnam War (1956–1975), American

These British soldiers in World War I were blinded by mustard gas released by the Germans on the battlefields of France. Both sides repeatedly used chemical weapons during the war. It was the first time such agents had been deployed on a wide scale.

An Accidental Terrorist?

Several gray areas confuse the issue of chemical and biological terrorism. For instance, certain events might be considered acts of crime by some, accidents by others.

The strange case of Typhoid Mary illustrates the complex issues surrounding the existence of chemicals and microorganisms as possible instruments of death. Mary Mallon was employed as a cook by a wealthy New York family in 1906. Soon after she started her job, family and staff members began to come down with typhoid fever. On investigation, it was found that Mallon had served in several previous households that had become inflicted with typhoid fever, resulting in at least one death. In coming years, Mallon was connected with other typhoid deaths, simply by working as a servant. Eventually, it was determined that she was a typhoid carrier. That is, she never suffered from typhoid fever herself, but the contagious disease was in her system and was passed on to residents of the homes where she served.

Few people today would call Mary Mallon a terrorist. Some, however, would argue that when she realized she might be posing a threat to society, she should have stopped being a cook. But what else could she do for a living? She continued to work as a cook and servant, exposing herself to unsuspecting households.

forces used an herbicide called Agent Orange to kill jungle plants and thus deprive enemy guerrilla fighters of their cover. The chemical was not intended to injure humans, but both U.S. veterans and Vietnamese citizens later claimed Agent Orange and similar poisons that were used during the conflict caused them health problems.

Napalm bombs explode in Vietnam in 1962. American forces used napalm to attack enemy Viet Cong fighters who concealed themselves in the thick forests. The infernos destroyed many acres of woodland.

Americans in Vietnam also used napalm, a chemical warhead that caused intense fires and stripped trees of their foliage. The United States had first employed napalm against the Japanese during World War II (1939–1945) in Pacific jungle island fighting. They found that by destroying the thick forest growth, they could expose the enemy. Other countries since then have used napalm in localized conflicts. Although it has been condemned by many because of the horrible effects it can have on humans, napalm today is in the arsenals of many nations' military forces.

Types of Biological Weapons

The following is a description of some of the kinds of biological weapons and their effects:

- **Anthrax,** a bacterial disease caused by *Bacillus anthracis,* is a biological agent that caused a panic in the United States in the autumn of 2001. This was shortly after the aerial terrorist attacks against the World Trade Center in New York City and the Pentagon near Washington, D.C. Tiny anthrax shells, or spores, can be fatal if inhaled, eaten, or touched to a skin wound—even in tiny amounts. When eaten, anthrax first produces symptoms resembling food poisoning. If inhaled, it causes difficulty breathing. Both types of exposure can be fatal. Military experts believe that if it could be distributed effectively, a small quantity of anthrax could destroy the population of a major city. However, while cultivating anthrax is not difficult, developing it in weapon form is.

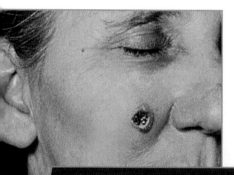

A tiny amount of anthrax caused this deep sore on the victim's face. If inhaled or swallowed, anthrax must be treated immediately or it may be fatal.

- **Ricin,** a poisonous protein extracted from castor beans, has been used as a biological weapon. Analysts are especially concerned about it for two reasons. First, castor beans, which make castor oil, are produced agriculturally in large quantities. Second, there is no known antidote to ricin, although exposure to it is not always fatal. Fever and acute intestinal disorders are initial symptoms. Eventually, respiratory failure and collapsing blood vessels can result in death.

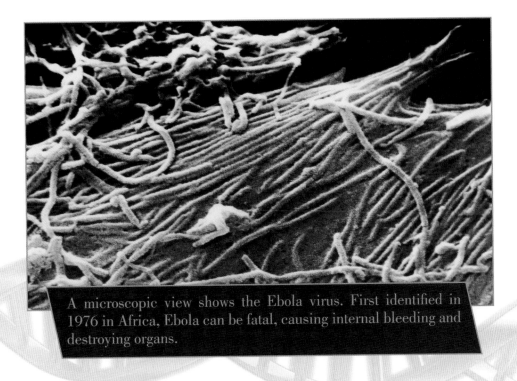

A microscopic view shows the Ebola virus. First identified in 1976 in Africa, Ebola can be fatal, causing internal bleeding and destroying organs.

- **Salmonella** has been used to poison food. *Salmonella* is a bacterium that can cause an infection in humans called salmonellosis.
- **Botulinum neurotoxin (BT)**, a disease caused by a bacterium *(Clostridium botulinum)* found in the soil, can be paralyzing and fatal. Botulism contamination can occur in food and drinks, and investigators believe terrorists theoretically could produce it as an aerosol. It would be difficult to accomplish, however. No effective terrorist or warfare attacks involving BT have occurred, but terrorists in Japan are known to have attempted it.

Other germs have interested military scientists and terrorists alike. For example, scientists believe it is possible to develop the Ebola virus into a weapon, but it apparently has never been used. The Ebola virus, which first produces flulike symptoms, is fatal in most cases, causing internal bleeding and organ damage.

Most chemicals in the air can be smelled and/or seen. The threat of biological attack is far more disturbing because most of these agents cannot be smelled or seen. They enter the human body just as natural diseases do. It may take days for them to multiply and produce symptoms of illness. Therefore, victims of biological warfare may not even realize they have been attacked until it is too late for effective treatment.

CBW researchers and analysts have observed that over the course of history, diseases have killed many times more humans than wars have. That is why the possibility of a large-scale biological attack is more worrisome than nuclear war to some security officials. Small-scale biological acts by terrorists are also deeply troubling because many terrorist organizations around the world are known to be experimenting with them.

Chapter Two

CHEMICAL AND BIOLOGICAL WARFARE THROUGHOUT HISTORY

During World War I, near the border between France and Belgium, the German army introduced the modern era of chemical warfare in April 1915. With the wind at their backs, army engineers opened almost six thousand containers of yellow-green chlorine gas. It blew over the entrenchments of opposing Allied forces, choking them and killing several thousand. The gas cloud was so terrifying that the Allies fled the field and the Germans themselves were able to advance only a short distance.

It was the first time harmful chemicals had been unleashed against a wartime foe on a large scale. The Germans continued to use several types of chemicals during World War I, including mustard

German soldiers send poison gas downwind, into the trenches of opposing soldiers, during World War I. Although widely used, poison gas was an unpredictable weapon; a wind shift could turn it back toward the attackers.

gas, which affects the skin. The Allies retaliated with chemical weapons of their own. By 1916, artillery units were firing gas-filled shells. Some two dozen chemicals were used by different armies, and others were being developed. In the end, more than a million soldiers and civilians are believed to have died as a result of chemicals during that war.

MYTHS AND FACTS

MYTH The touch of a microscopic speck of anthrax to the skin is fatal.

FACT If treated promptly, anthrax on the skin is almost never fatal. The most deadly form of anthrax contamination is by inhalation.

MYTH Different terrorist organizations are using CBWs almost daily in different parts of the world.

FACT Although many terrorist groups are known to possess hazardous chemicals and organisms, the actual use of them has been rare.

MYTH CBWs are relatively new forms of warfare.

FACT Fighting with poisoned arrows, the deliberate spreading of plagues, and other forms of chemical and biological aggression have occurred for thousands of years.

This was not the first time chemicals had been considered as weapons. The Fenians, an Irish independence group, plotted to spray poison gas into the British House of Commons during the 1870s but did not carry it out. Military experimenters tested poison gas during the Boer War (1899–1902) in South Africa and the Russo-Japanese War (1904–1905).

Actually, the use of CBWs goes back much further. According to tradition, Hercules, the early Greek hero, used poisoned arrows

Flying Vipers

Many people are terrified of snakes. It does not matter to them whether the creature is venomous and poses a physical threat. The appearance of any serpent makes them withdraw in fright.

Imagine what it would be like to have a snake zoom in from nowhere and land at your feet—not just any kind of snake, but one with a deadly bite. Ancient battle strategists understood the paralyzing fear that such an occurrence would produce in an opposing force.

The use of arrowheads dipped in deadly venom has been practiced by many fighters over the centuries, from small African and South American tribes to sophisticated Greek legions. At times, warriors attacked not just with venomous arrows but with the vipers themselves. In the third century BCE, Hannibal, the Carthaginian conqueror, reportedly had his sailors hurl jars containing snakes onto the decks of an opposing naval fleet. The pandemonium it produced helped him win the battle.

In Afghanistan around 1000 CE, Islamic invaders catapulted mysterious, bulky sacks into Sistan, a fortress under siege. These sacks also contained snakes, producing the same chaotic effect as that inflicted by Hannibal thirteen centuries before.

against his enemies—and died after putting on a poisoned cloak. These stories are called myths, but most myths are rooted in grains of reality. Obviously, the chroniclers of ancient mythology understood about poisoned weapons.

Horrors of History

Besides the Greeks, different tribes of natives on different continents have fought with poison-tipped arrows. In time, warriors also found ways to spread disease—an early form of a biological weapon. During the fourteenth century, Tartar invaders literally catapulted the corpses of plague victims inside the walls of a fortress they were besieging. Some historians suspect this may have resulted in the spread of the bubonic plague, known as the Black Death, throughout Europe, killing a third of the continent's population. Four hundred years later, British soldiers reportedly gave Native Americans, as a peace offering, blankets contaminated by smallpox.

Poisoned arrows, corpses, and blankets were crude weapons compared to some of the sophisticated devices of modern times. But they were no less terrifying and deadly to their victims then as newer forms of chemical and biological warfare are now.

The examples from history are numerous. Folklorist Adrienne Mayor, who investigated ancient methods of warfare for her book *Greek Fire*, observes that while most armies engaged in what might be considered civilized warfare, many of them fought "outside the rules." If folktales handed down in their cultures are to be believed, they drugged their enemies' water wells and coated arrowheads with snake venom. When possible, they maneuvered so that their foes were forced to camp in boggy areas swarming with mosquitoes. They sent people dying with contagious diseases into opposing camps and communities. They hurled payloads of serpents, scorpions, and wasp nests into opponents' forts, ships, and battle lines.

Even food could be used as a lethal weapon. Some 2,500 years ago, Greek soldiers devoured wild honey in what is now Turkey and were rendered insane and helpless for several days. Military strategists began leaving poisoned food and wine for their enemies to find. A leader who was particularly fascinated by the

Pontiac, chief of the Ottawa people, angrily accuses European soldiers of spreading smallpox among his tribe by giving them infected blankets in 1764. Other crude forms of biological warfare occurred many centuries earlier.

use of poison was King Mithridates VI Eupator of Pontus (120–60 BCE). Besides being a military commander, he was a toxicologist who experimented extensively with poisons and antidotes. They were his favorite weapons for eliminating personal enemies, who included his mother and other close relatives. He tried new concoctions on prisoners to observe their effects. Ironically, when Mithridates tried to poison himself after a military defeat, he failed because his body had become immune to his own toxins. He ordered a soldier to kill him with a sword.

In India and China, ancient military engineers experimented with poisonous smoke clouds. During the seventh century, navies in the Middle East began using a weapon known as Greek fire. It was a chemical mixture that burned even on the surface of the sea. For hundreds of years, it proved effective in repelling invading fleets.

Devious Weapons of the Twentieth Century

Massive volumes of chemicals were being tested for warfare by the turn of the twentieth century and were used with terrible effect in World War I. Spanish forces used them to put down a revolt in its northern African colony of Morocco during the 1920s. The Italian army used poison gas when it invaded Ethiopia to create the Italian East Africa Colony in 1935–1936.

Biological weapons came later. Scientists began to experiment with them widely during the 1930s. When it occupied China in 1937–1938, the Japanese army used chemical weapons against resistance fighters. Japan also began to develop biological weapons. Its air force allegedly dropped grain and insects contaminated with plague-causing bacteria on Chinese towns. During World War II (1939–1945), Japanese researchers experimented on Chinese and Russian prisoners of war and on civilians to

An elderly man in China still suffers from germ warfare carried out by the Japanese army in World War II. His legs were injured permanently by an anthrax infection.

learn how certain diseases could be spread effectively throughout an enemy army or population. Diseases that interested them included smallpox, typhoid fever, tuberculosis, tetanus, and others. In the last months of the war, Japan was preparing to drop masses of disease-carrying fleas on American forces in the Pacific but was unable to carry out the plan.

Japan's ally Germany, interestingly, amassed great stockpiles of sarin and tabun weapons but did not deploy them in World War II. There were several reasons. The way the war unfolded, the Germans did not find a practical use for them. They also feared that retaliation by their opponents could be more destructive than their own attacks. Some historians believe Adolf Hitler, the German leader, personally opposed using toxic weapons because he knew firsthand the agony they could cause. As a German army corporal during World War I, Hitler was temporarily blinded by mustard gas and was injured so severely that he had to be hospitalized.

The German military slaughtered millions of Jews and other prisoners in extermination and concentration camps during World War II. Most of the victims died from gas poisoning. A gas container is pictured here.

It should be noted that German Nazis did use poison gases to kill prisoners in concentration camps.

After World War II, some of the German and Japanese biological weapon scientists went to work for the governments of other nations, including the United States.

Chapter Three

WHY DO PEOPLE FIGHT THIS WAY?

Most people believe there is a difference between fair and unfair fighting. In a fair, or ethical, contest, opponents use the same weapons and fight the same way. The side that is more powerful or that uses a smarter strategy wins. Conflicts are unfair, or unethical, most agree, when one side resorts to weapons and tactics that may hurt not only opposing warriors but society at large. Nuclear, chemical, and biological weapons are considered unethical, mainly because they are uncontrollable. They may injure or kill thousands, even millions of people who are not involved in the fighting. Computer viruses are regarded as unethical for much the same reason. Millions of victims worldwide—all classes of people—suffer pointlessly from them.

After World War I, the nations of the world reached agreements to curb warfare and aggression and specifically to ban chemical and biological warfare. These League of Nation delegates met in 1923.

International efforts to curb the use of CBWs date to 1925. The Geneva Protocol was adopted by the League of Nations in response to the use of deadly gases by the German army and other forces during World War I. It prohibited poison gas and biological weapons in international conflicts. Signed by almost 150 nations, it showed clearly that people everywhere were appalled by the horrors of biochemical warfare.

This was an unusual treaty. For many centuries, wars had been waged with swords, rifles, cannons, and bombs—and occasionally with secret weapons such as poisons. Whenever the warring powers became weary, or when one side was overwhelmed or became distracted by other problems, treaties were arranged to end the fighting. The opposing sides divided up territory and property, exchanged prisoners, and agreed to other terms. Life went on.

Unlike previous agreements, the Geneva Protocol was not arranged to end a war. It was signed to outlaw the use of certain types of weapons in all future wars. People across the globe recognized that in an imperfect world, fighting is inevitable. At the same time, certain forms of fighting, they decided, should be forbidden.

The Geneva Protocol failed to prevent chemical and biological warfare. Many nations continued to make those kinds of weapons and to develop new varieties. A few actually used them. They did not deploy them on an all-out scale, though. To this day, the major world powers have been afraid to use CBWs against one another. For one thing, they fear a powerful backlash of world opinion. They also fear that the use of CBWs probably would lead to escalation, possibly even to a nuclear holocaust. Besides, they see little advantage in using CBWs as long as tried-and-tested weapons serve their purposes.

But today, a new brand of military force has arisen—and it is not afraid to use unethical weapons. Terrorist groups—some motivated by politics, others by religious fanaticism—have demonstrated a willingness to hurt and kill civilians, including their own people, for the sake of achieving their objectives. Many terrorist organizations are very small, consisting of only a few dozen militants. Others are formidable in size, with thousands of members operating in different places. Some, like Al Qaeda, are actually networks of different terrorist groups operating loosely together all over the world. By using CBWs and other unconventional weapons, they can cause widespread panic and, in turn, affect the politics and economies of world powers.

Civilized Versus Uncivilized Warfare

During the Cold War, both the United States and the Soviet Union developed arsenals of chemical and biological weapons. They never used them against each other, though, because both superpowers knew that their deployment undoubtedly would trigger a nuclear war. In effect, it could bring about the end of civilization

U.S. military workers carefully handle chemical-laden rockets. The weapons were destroyed in compliance with an agreement reached by many nations during the 1990s.

as people know it. They realized only third world militant regimes might gain political advantages by using CBW arsenals.

Even before the Cold War, most international powers thought better of launching biochemical attacks, even if they possessed CBWs. They realized many people could be killed and injured, and neither side had much to gain from it.

International terrorist organizations, on the other hand, have little fear of retaliation. Many of them have cells of operation in different villages, cities, and countries. They do not occupy specific territories that can be pinpointed on the globe, so they cannot become nuclear targets. They are shadowy, secretive organizations whose members lose themselves among the public at large. It is difficult for government forces to identify and locate them or to understand the scope of their activities.

Terrorist groups do not restrict their attacks to military targets. They frequently attack civilian populations of nations or cultural groups they consider their rivals. It is hard to stop them. Armed forces are trained and protected against the threat of CBWs. Civilians, though, are completely vulnerable.

Cheap and Easy Destruction

Easy to make, and hard to police: those are the two characteristics of chemical and biological weapons that make them attractive to terrorists and very troubling to law enforcement and security professionals. Terrorists can learn to make primitive CBWs using materials that are easily obtained.

Some of the chemicals that can be used as weapons are commonly sold as insecticides, rodent poisons, and cleaning agents. They can be bought by anyone at hardware stores and supermarkets. The problem for terrorists, experts agree, is not obtaining the ingredients. Rather, it is how to disseminate them to achieve the desired effects. When they are released into the natural world—the air or water reservoirs—nature itself (wind, rain, currents, etc.) diminishes their strength. Much depends on

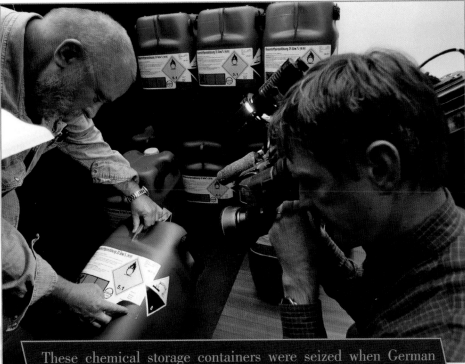

These chemical storage containers were seized when German police cracked a terrorist plot in 2005. The terrorists reportedly planned to attack a U.S. military base and a German airport.

circumstances, which quickly can change, and the attacker can become a victim.

Factors Involved in Developing and Deploying CBWs

If biochemical weapons are so easy to obtain, why haven't more attacks occurred? Several things must occur for a secret group or individual to deploy a CBW effectively. The substance must be obtained or cultivated in quantities vast enough to cause notable injuries and deaths. It must be isolated safely inside the lab so developers can work with it. And it requires a delivery system.

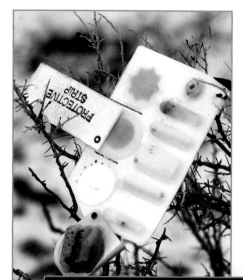

This testing kit at a military site in Utah can detect biological and chemical substances in the air. It is impossible, though, for such devices to identify every possible biochemical weapon.

Analysts emphasize that such weapons are extremely dangerous to handle. In fact, they pose at least as great a threat to the people experimenting with them as they pose to intended victims. Their use can backfire. Once they are disseminated, there is no way to control them. The end result might not be in the interest of those who released them.

For example, such an attack by a terrorist group could injure and kill friends of the terrorists as well as their opponents. It could also provoke a massive backlash from appalled third parties, people and governments who originally had no interest in either side of the conflict.

However, those who are bold enough to develop and use CBWs are formidable threats to society. Harmful chemicals and biological organisms can be set loose in hard-to-detect ways. While conducting tests during the mid-1950s, the U.S. Army demonstrated that they could be contained in lightbulbs and dropped and shattered on hard surfaces, or sprayed from aerosol containers from cars and boats. The Japanese terrorist cult that wrought havoc aboard subways in 1995 used another simple method: placing them inconspicuously in plastic bags, puncturing the bags, and escaping on foot as the gas began to spread.

In a U.S. military experiment forty years ago, a mock chemical attack reportedly was launched in the New York subway system. Fake anthrax powder was sprayed through ventilation systems and released from lightbulbs flung into dark subway tunnels. The rush of air accompanying the fast-moving trains pulled the "anthrax" from one subway station to another. Calculations of the spreading particles suggested that had it been real anthrax, it might have killed hundreds of thousands of subway riders.

On the other hand, CBW attacks may have no effect at all. It is possible that numerous attacks actually have occurred but have gone unnoticed because nothing happened.

Fanatic Perspectives

Many experts believe large-scale CBW attacks are likely to be carried out only by the most extreme radicals, those willing to cause chaos regardless of the costs to themselves. To suicide terrorists, it does not matter that their weapons could backfire—as long as they also succeed in the intended mission of harming the enemy. Many terrorists are not concerned by the possibility of hurting unintended victims either. They can justify their actions as long as they succeed in hurting their enemies and achieving their long-term goals.

Terrorists also understand that the panic caused by even a small-scale attack can cause more emotional, economic, and political damage than the attack itself. As early as the 1930s, analysts of chemical weapons pointed out that the major damage they cause would be psychological, not physical.

U.S. law enforcement officers are on the alert against attacks not just by terrorist organizations but by lone criminals acting from personal, often bizarre, motives. An example was the Alphabet Bomber, Muharem Kurbegovic, whose bombing at the Los Angeles International Airport in 1974 killed three people. After his arrest, police found in his apartment a large quantity of chemicals as well as gas masks, lab equipment, and manuals on biochemical weapons. Kurbegovic, who is serving a life prison sentence, threatened to carry out nerve gas attacks in Washington, D.C. What apparently triggered his anger was that Los Angeles officials had denied him a permit to open a dance hall.

Chapter Four

THE USE OF CHEMICAL AND BIOLOGICAL WEAPONS IN RECENT YEARS

erman terrorists in 1975 managed to steal mustard gas from a military site in West Germany. They vowed they would use it even against civilians in order to win their political objectives. Apparently, the threat was not carried out.

In the hands of certain power brokers during the last quarter century, though, aggression with CBWs has been more than a threat. In some instances, attacks have occurred with no warning.

Saddam Hussein's CBW Program

Iraq used mustard gas and other chemical weapons against neighboring Iran during their long border

Kurdish militia fighters in Iraq visit the mass grave of civilians who died in a gas attack in 1988. The victims were killed by order of their own president, Saddam Hussein.

warfare of the 1980s. Iran also reportedly used chemical weapons against Iraq, though its weapons program was more primitive and limited. Iraq's president, Saddam Hussein, ordered his military to use CBWs against citizens of their own country: Kurdish dissidents. Outside analysts estimate at least three thousand Kurds and some forty-five thousand Iranians perished as a result of Hussein's chemical weapons deployment.

After the Persian Gulf War in 1991, Iraq denied that it had used chemical weapons against the U.S.-led allied forces who defeated it. However, Czech and French soldiers trained in chemical weapons detection reported nerve and mustard gas in the southern border area where the allies were staging for battle. American forces reported a mysterious explosion over their encampment. A thick gas cloud descended, some said,

A U.S. veteran shows some of the medications he takes daily to relieve pain. He is disabled from Gulf War syndrome combined with injuries he suffered during the conflict in the early 1990s.

burning skin and causing breathing difficulty.

Within months after the war ended, thousands of allied soldiers began suffering mysterious illness symptoms—intestinal disorders, unexplained fatigue, memory loss, skin rashes, and joint pain. Some of the cases of what became known as Gulf War syndrome were severe, rendering the veterans unable to work. Eventually, the U.S. government acknowledged that several hundred thousand military personnel may have been affected by sarin. The poisonous gas reportedly was released in an uncontrollable cloud after a vast Iraqi ammunition depot exploded.

No one could be sure how many of the cases attributed to Gulf War syndrome actually resulted from chemical contamination. Some health specialists suspected that smoke from oil wells torched by retreating Iraqi soldiers was partially to blame. Others pointed out that it is not uncommon for wartime stress to cause long-lasting health problems. Other suggested causes

A United Nations weapons team works to remove sarin-filled rockets found in Iraq after the Gulf War. Despite UN efforts, many observers believe Saddam Hussein continued to maintain a secret stockpile of banned weapons.

included certain medications given to allied soldiers in an attempt to ward off chemicals and germs.

After the Gulf War, the United Nations required President Hussein to demolish his weapons of mass destruction. UN inspectors found sophisticated Iraqi facilities for making weapons to launch anthrax and nerve gas attacks. Iraq cleverly concealed its biochemical laboratories. When Hussein's son-in-law defected in 1995, he turned over to Western authorities documents revealing the extent of the secret program. Many weapons and factories were destroyed, but foreign military analysts were convinced Hussein never fully dismantled his CBW program. This concern was a key motive for the 2003 invasion of Iraq by U.S., British, and other international forces, toppling the Hussein regime.

Iraq is one of many countries where evidence of biochemical weapons development has concerned foreign governments. Libya's military leader, Colonel Muammar Qaddafi, has long been known to support terrorist activities based in various Islamic countries. His military built underground laboratories that quickly could be disguised as ordinary pharmaceutical facilities to deceive foreign inspectors. Qaddafi's links to terrorist acts prompted punishment from the international community, including air raids by the United States. Since the 1990s, though, Qaddafi has shown a willingness to abandon his nation's WMD development and normalize interactions with Western governments. In 2006, after years of international sanctions and isolation, the United States renewed diplomatic relations with Libya.

Chemical and Biological Weapons Elsewhere

Aum Shinrikyo, a radical Japanese cult, was responsible for a deadly chemical gas attack in Japanese subways in 1995. Cult terrorists deposited plastic bags of it on three commuter trains in the Tokyo subway system, then released the gas by piercing the bags with umbrella tips. Thousands were injured; twelve died. Police who broke up the terrorist operation discovered large stockpiles of chemicals as well as biological agents. Apparently, the cult leader's ultimate intention was to attack Japanese government buildings and a U.S. naval base, provoking an international crisis.

In 1984, cult followers of Bhagwan Shree Rajneesh poisoned salad bars at restaurants in a small Oregon town. They used

A Deadly Dose of Sarin

Invisible gas filtered through a midnight train from Yokohama to Tokyo, Japan, in March 1995. Eleven people were hospitalized, complaining of nausea, blurred vision, and headaches. No one died, but it was the herald of a far more sinister attack that caused panic among Japan's millions of rail travelers.

Later that month, twelve people died and more than three thousand were sickened when sarin, a nerve gas, was released from plastic bags of liquid placed in several Tokyo subway trains during the morning rush period. As the trains came to a stop, terrified, retching passengers swarmed out the doors. Many of them collapsed on station platforms. Two of the fatalities were subway workers who entered a poisoned train to locate and clean up one of the punctured gas containers. Two major subways and more than two dozen stations were closed. Police learned that the attacks were the work of a terrorist cult called Aum Shinrikyo.

Sarin (isopropyl methylphosphonofluoridate) can be dangerous in gas or liquid form. It can kill an unprotected victim in a matter of minutes. At first, the victim experiences watery eyes and profuse sweating. Vomiting and severe headaches follow. If not immediately treated, the poisoning can paralyze muscles and render the person unable to breathe.

Salmonella bacteria, which causes severe digestive problems if eaten. Approximately 750 diners were sickened, but no one died. The cult's apparent motive was to disrupt an upcoming election.

This was the only wide-scale biological attack in the United States until September 2001. One week after Al Qaeda terrorists

REWARD
UP TO $2,500,000

For information leading to the arrest and conviction of the individual(s) responsible for the mailing of letters containing anthrax to the New York Post, Tom Brokaw at NBC, Senator Tom Daschle and Senator Patrick Leahy:

AS A RESULT OF EXPOSURE TO ANTHRAX, FIVE (5) PEOPLE HAVE DIED.

The person responsible for these deaths…

- Likely has a scientific background/work history which may include a specific familiarity with anthrax

- Has a level of comfort in and around the Trenton, NJ area due to present or prior association

Anyone having information, contact **America's Most Wanted** at **1-800-CRIME TV** or the **FBI** via e-mail at **amerithrax@fbi.gov**

All information will be held in strict confidence. Reward payment will be made in accordance with the conditions of Postal Service Reward Notice 296, dated February 2000. Source of reward funds: US Postal Service and FBI $2,000,000; ADVO, Inc. $500,000.

A U.S. Postal Service reward poster shows four envelopes that contained anthrax. They were mailed in 2001 to prominent journalists and U.S. senators.

hijacked airliners and destroyed the World Trade Center in New York, mysterious letters began to be received at the offices of several news organizations and U.S. senators. The letters contained anthrax spores. Five people died and about two dozen suffered from exposure. The last mailings occurred the following month. No arrests were ever made.

Ricin-contaminated mail has also been found in recent years in various postal facilities. One letter in 2003 was addressed to the White House. In February 2008, vials of ricin were found in a Las Vegas hotel room, two weeks after Roger Von Bergendorff, the man renting the room, was hospitalized. Bergendorff eventually recovered from ricin exposure and was charged with illegal possession of both biological and chemical weapons.

These and other news accounts suggest widespread experimentation with dangerous chemicals and microorganisms by individuals as well as terrorist groups. Criminals are not the only known users of such substances, though. Government security organizations have developed and used biochemical devices in secret operations. Russia's secret police force has reportedly employed ricin as a tool for assassination, using umbrellas tipped with it to gouge victims.

Security officials in major nations fear that smaller countries' governments, as well as well-funded terrorist cell groups and networks, are hiring chemists and biologists who helped develop CBWs for superpowers. Western authorities suspect that scientists who worked for the former Soviet Union have been lured away by militant governments and organizations in the Middle East, Asia, and elsewhere.

Al Qaeda, the notorious international terrorist network responsible for the September 11, 2001, attacks on the United States, has long been known to experiment with biological and chemical weapons. It was founded by Osama bin Laden, whose mission is to oust U.S. and other Western influences from Islamic countries. In December 2000, Italian and German police apprehended Al Qaeda operatives who planned to attack the European Parliament

Wearing a Hazmat protective suit, an emergency worker in Utah investigates the home of a man found in possession of ricin. The suspect was hospitalized for nine weeks after being contaminated himself.

building in France. The terrorists' weapon of choice in that case was sarin. Al Qaeda has tested other chemicals, including cyanide, and biological agents such as anthrax, salmonella, and botulinum bacteria.

In the aftermath of September 11, 2001, the United States and other governments launched a global campaign to quash terrorism in general and Al Qaeda in particular. Thousands of alleged Al Qaeda members have been arrested, and many of the network's leaders have been killed. Some wonder, though, whether the war against terrorism can be won. While Al Qaeda is the most notorious terrorist organization, it is just one of many.

Chapter Five

COPING WITH THE THREAT

Many Americans wonder why terrorists have not made frequent and massive CBW attacks. Could it be that even cold-blooded militants have a conscience and refrain from the use of these weapons for moral reasons? Government officials and military analysts doubt it, but they note that deploying chemical and biological weapons is not such a simple matter.

First, CBWs are risky to make. Explosions or leaks during the manufacture of chemical weapons can turn the attack on the attackers. Biological weapons are likewise dangerous to handle. The greatest problem for their developers is finding effective ways to direct the germs against an intended target without affecting neighboring populations.

Because of the unpredictable and potentially catastrophic nature of CBWs, governments have tried to control them for the last hundred years.

Agreements to Ban Chemical and Biological Weapons

During the early 1900s, world political leaders became concerned by the potential for using chemical weapons in the recent Boer and Russo-Japanese wars. Delegates to an international peace conference at The Hague, The Netherlands, in 1907 agreed to certain rules of acceptable warfare. Among other things, they forbade the use of tear gas and similar chemicals. Less than ten years later, opposing armies in World War I flagrantly ignored the treaty, and the age of chemical warfare began.

The Geneva Protocol of 1925 forbade the use of both chemical and biological weapons. Its effectiveness, too, was debatable. Within fifteen years, Japan and Germany were developing and using new CBWs, and other nations were experimenting with them.

In modern times, many countries agreed to the Biological Weapons Convention of 1972 and the Chemical Weapons Convention of 1993. These agreements go further than banning the use of such weapons; they forbid governments from developing and stockpiling them. But again, observers question their effectiveness. Some nations refused to sign the international agreements, and some that did sign are suspected of violating the conventions.

The status of stockpiled chemical weapons by major governments is unknown. Despite the Chemical Weapons Convention of 1993 and pledges to incinerate national military stockpiles, some worry that portions of the old arsenals are secretly being retained and that CBWs continue to be developed by military scientists.

During the twentieth century, the United States reportedly amassed about 30 metric tons (33 short tons) of chemicals for possible military use. The former Soviet Union is believed to have

These stockpiled chemicals await disposal at a weapons storage site in Russia. Russia sought assistance from the United States to carry out the expensive disposal process.

stockpiled much more. Both countries agreed to the Chemical Weapons Conventions treaty, and the U.S. military is known to have incinerated (burned) large chemical stores. Another way to dispose of them is to mix them with other chemicals that make them harmless. Each process is very expensive and must be carried out with extreme caution to prevent polluting the environment.

Some Western observers believe China, North Korea, Iran, and other countries continue to develop and maintain chemical weapons.

As for biological weapons, U.S. officials suspect that Russia, China, North Korea, Iran, Israel, Egypt, and several other nations have secret biological weapons programs. Countries that do comply

The Sverdlovsk Disaster

In 1972, the United States, the Soviet Union, and Great Britain agreed to stop biological warfare research and stockpiling. They signed an agreement to that effect called the Biological Weapons Convention. It later became apparent, however, that the Soviets were secretly continuing their CBW program. In 1979 came chilling reports of an anthrax outbreak in Sverdlovsk, a city in Russia's Ural Mountains. Sverdlovsk was known to be the home of top-secret Soviet military programs. Some sixty civilians died from anthrax poisoning; Western observers believe many more military personnel also succumbed. For years, the Soviet government maintained that the tragedy was caused by meat contamination. Only in 1992, after the breakup of the Soviet Union into different countries, did the government of Russia admit what outsiders had long suspected: anthrax bacteria had accidentally escaped from a biological weapons research site.

The Sverdlovsk catastrophe illustrated two things: that some governments are continuing to develop CBWs, despite international treaties, and that these chemical and biological agents are exceptionally dangerous—even to those who would use them.

with agreements to dispose of their germ arsenals have been able to destroy most of them with disinfectants and ultraviolet light. Certain organisms, though, cannot be eliminated so easily.

As the threat of terrorist activities heightened at the turn of the century, one proposal was to make CBW possession a crime under international law. Skeptics doubted it would thwart the activities of terrorists, who have shown no regard for international treaties, morals, or ethics. And making an ironclad case against a suspected user of CBWs could be very difficult.

Problems and Suspicions

The episode of Gulf War syndrome after the 1991 conflict pointed out some of the problems with preventing and investigating CBW threats. Thousands of allied veterans were convinced after the war that exposure to chemicals was the cause of various long-term health problems they experienced. Some officials, however, believed at least some of the ailments resulted from other causes. Many mysterious illnesses have occurred throughout history. In certain cases, the sources have never been positively identified. Furthermore, it can be difficult to prove that these types of outbreaks result from intentional attacks.

The uncertain nature of chemical and biological threats raises a chilling suspicion. Could seemingly natural disease epidemics and pandemics such as influenza be started by bioterrorists? Scientists believe no flu viruses have ever been used as weapons, although the Spanish flu of 1918–1919 seemed questionable, in the minds of some at the time, because it came at the end of the first great war involving CBW attacks. That pandemic killed more than twenty million people. Medical researchers today believe it is conceivable for terrorists to obtain and develop lab samples of strains of epidemic diseases.

Understandably, many people ponder the causes of recent food scares, especially instances of contaminated fish and other products imported from foreign countries.

Protection from Chemicals and Other Agents

Gas masks became standard trench warfare equipment after the Germans began using chemical weapons in 1915. Today, soldiers and law enforcement officers in high-risk areas have complete biohazard outfits that cover them completely, from head to foot, and include filtered breathing mechanisms.

New Jersey National Guard soldiers participate in an emergency drill. The exercise was at the site of a building theoretically contaminated with harmful biochemicals.

The issue of protective outfits is one resistance measure that can be taken in the face of immediate exposure to CBWs. A fundamental shortcoming is that even where protective clothing is available, by the time targeted victims put it on, exposure may have already occurred. It is useful mainly to outside military and emergency workers who know they will be entering a dangerous area.

In civilian areas, health services monitoring provides one line of defense. Another is modern purification technology used in city water systems, which can prevent or lessen human contamination by poisons.

The key to protecting a large target population is early detection. Modern military forces use chemical detection devices in combat zones, but these are not common in civilian areas. Even if they were, they would be effective only against chemical, not biological, threats. By the time victims realize they are under biological attack and identify the harmful agent, massive damage has already occurred. Although military scientists have created systems to monitor the air for traces of anthrax and other bio-weapons, they cannot detect every type of germ.

It is possible—but impractical—to construct special, airtight shelters with self-contained ventilation and survival essentials. The drawbacks are obvious. Facilities big enough to accommodate large populations would be extremely expensive to construct, and their effectiveness would be questionable. Small shelters for units of soldiers in combat areas are useful for protection, but they impose self-imprisonment on the fighting forces.

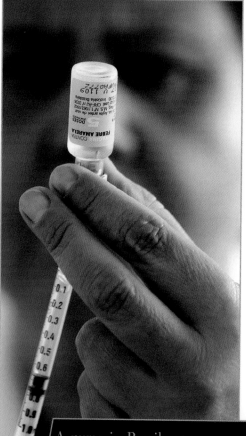

A nurse in Brazil prepares a yellow fever vaccine. Travelers in Brazil's inland forests were urged to receive vaccinations after several deaths were attributed to the disease.

Once contamination has occurred, it can often be counter-acted by simple washing, if it is limited to the surface of the skin and is treated quickly. If chemicals or germs have invaded the body, medical treatment is required. Antibiotics are available to combat most biological agents, but immediate care is vital because some CBWs can cause death within minutes.

Ideally, people in danger of exposure will be prepared. Plagues spread by biological organisms can usually be prevented or treated. Vaccinations have long been effective in curbing smallpox, for example. More recently, vaccines have been developed to counter anthrax and newer organisms. The U.S. Food and Drug Administration (FDA) approved an anthrax vaccination forty years ago. Since then, it has been given to millions of military personnel as well as to certain researchers, farmers, and others who could be exposed to the bacteria either accidentally or deliberately.

Additional vaccines against other microorganisms have been developed, but who should receive them? How many people? The idea of trying to inoculate everyone against every possible biological threat is ridiculous, especially because new germ strains frequently emerge, resistant to all previous vaccinations.

Most observers believe the main deterrent to the use of CBWs is ethical concern. If national military departments and terrorist organizations are persuaded that the use of these weapons will bring down withering retaliation, they will think twice.

Conclusion

In the aftermath of the terrorist attacks against the United States on September 11, 2001, the U.S. government established the federal Department of Homeland Security (DHS). Its purpose is to thwart terrorist efforts, protect the citizenry, and oversee recovery in the event of future attacks.

DHS workers carry out their tasks on four fronts. The intelligence division monitors the activities of known and suspected terrorist organizations and analyzes reports of security threats. The border and transportation division seeks to prevent foreign terrorists from entering the country and to make the nation's highways, airways, and sea lanes safe. The science and technology division researches specific types of terrorist weapons—chemical and biological as well as nuclear. The emergency preparedness and response division is organized to coordinate recovery efforts by different agencies.

Several existing government agencies were placed under the direction of the Department of Homeland Security. They include the Secret Service, responsible for protecting the president and other high-ranking officials; the U.S. Coast Guard; the U.S. Customs Service; the Federal Emergency Management Agency; the Transportation Security Administration; and the Bureau of Citizenship and Immigration Services. In addition, various federal and state intelligence agencies—including the Federal Bureau of Investigation, Central Intelligence Agency, and National Security Agency—work in close support of the DHS.

Despite the creation of such a large security organization, public fears remain, not only of terrorist plots but of the massive development of CBWs by superpowers. Some Western officials believe the Russian military has been developing a system for delivering biological warheads to targets thousands of miles away via long-range missiles.

Even though these weapons and the technology to disperse them exist, some analysts doubt they will ever be used to inflict heavy casualties. Terrorists, they understand, do not need to carry out major CBW attacks. Small, isolated incidents can create panic, which, in turn, can trigger political changes in the leadership and policies of enemy governments. These much simpler, easier attacks can serve their purposes just as well as a single major attack.

It may also be comforting, in a way, to remember that CBWs are not new threats. Humankind's ancient ancestors feared them perhaps as much as people do today. These kinds of weapons have worried soldiers and civilians throughout recorded history.

Consider this fatal possibility: "He'll go to Ephyre and get deadly poisons to put in our wine-bowl and kill us all." That dire alarm was expressed by the Greek poet Homer in the *Odyssey*, written almost three thousand years ago.

GLOSSARY

aerosol A gas spray or cloud.

anoxia The shortage or absence of oxygen in the bloodstream.

antibiotic A type of medicine that can prevent or kill a harmful microorganism in the body.

antidote A specific type of treatment for poisoning.

binary (compound) chemical A new chemical produced from the combining of two or more other chemicals.

bubonic plague A dealy bacterial plague that causes a swelling of lymph glands.

cell group A small, local unit of a network or international organization.

Cold War The period of tension, lasting from the end of World War II to 1990, between the Soviet Bloc and Western nations led by the United States.

contaminate To poison food, water, or other essentials.

convention An agreement among nations.

conventional weapons Tools of fighting that have been used for a long time, ranging from ancient spears and arrows to gunpowder and bombs.

dissident One who opposes established policies or majority opinions.

enzyme A protein that can cause a biochemical reaction.

epidemic A widespread outbreak of a disease in a particular region or country.

ethics When applied to warfare, the debate over which systems are acceptable; generally, weapons that could harm large civilian populations as well as military forces are considered unethical.

herbicide A substance that is used to destroy harmful plants.

inoculate To vaccinate; to administer a drug for the purpose of preventing a specific illness.

microorganism A living being so small that it can be seen only with a microscope.

pandemic An outbreak of a disease that spreads to other countries or around the globe.

pathogen A microorganism that can cause a disease.

payload, warhead The part of a weapon that contains explosives or harmful chemicals or organisms.

protocol A negotiated document that outlines general terms of a treaty or an agreement.

respiratory system The nose, lung, and other parts of the body that take in and distribute oxygen.

sanctions Economic restrictions imposed on a country that is violating international law or accepted ethical or moral standards.

stockpile An accumulated supply of weapons or other products.

tactics Methods of fighting.

toxicologist An expert in poisons and antidotes.

unconventional weapons Devices of warfare used secretly or in defiance of accepted practices; examples include nuclear, chemical, and biological weapons.

weapons of mass destruction (WMDs) Weapons that will affect not only military forces but large civilian populations as well.

FOR MORE INFORMATION

Agency for Healthcare Research and Quality
U.S. Department of Health and Human Services
540 Gaither Road
Rockville, MD 20850
(301) 427-1364
Web site: http://www.ahrq.gov
This agency's Web site section on "Public Health Emergency
    Preparedness" includes a Bioterrorism and Emerging
    Infections category.

Canadian Security Intelligence Service
P.O. Box 9732, Station T
Ottawa, ON K1G 4G4
Canada
(613) 993-9620
Web site: http://www.csis-scrs.gc.ca
This service collects and analyzes security information in
    Canada and abroad to advise the Canadian government.

Center for Biosecurity
University of Pittsburgh Medical Center
Pier IV Building
621 E. Pratt Street, Suite 210
Baltimore, MD 21202
(443) 573-3304
Web site: http://www.upmc-biosecurity.org
This center provides details about chemical agents and diseases,
    as well as information about security policies and programs.

Centers for Disease Control and Prevention (CDC)
U.S. Department of Health and Human Services

1600 Clifton Road
Atlanta, GA 30333
(800) 311-3435 or (404) 498-1515
Web site: http://www.cdc.gov
The CDC's "Emergency Preparedness & Response" Web site
    section contains information on chemical emergencies and
    bioterrorism.

Central Intelligence Agency (CIA)
Office of Public Affairs
Washington, DC 20505
(703) 482-0623
Web site: http://www.cia.gov
The CIA is the federal government's independent agency for
    providing security information to senior policy makers.

Federal Bureau of Investigation (FBI)
J. Edgar Hoover Building
935 Pennsylvania Avenue NW
Washington, DC 20535-0001
Web site: http://www.fbi.gov
See particularly the FBI's Web site section on counterterrorism
    (http://www.fbi.gov/terrorinfo/counterrorism/
    waronterrorhome.htm).

The Henry L. Stimson Center
1111 19th Street NW, 12th Floor
Washington, DC 20036
(202) 223-5956
Web site: http://www.stimson.org
This is a nonprofit, nonpartisan organization whose priorities
    include reducing weapons of mass destruction.

The James Martin Center for Nonproliferation Studies
Monterey Institute of International Studies

460 Pierce Street
Monterey, CA 93940
(831) 647-4154
Web site: http://cns.miis.edu
This center seeks to "combat the spread of weapons of mass
 destruction (WMD) by training the next generation of nonproliferation specialists and disseminating timely information
 and analysis."

National Institute of Allergies and Infectious Diseases
National Institutes of Health
NIAID Office of Communication and Government Relations
6610 Rockledge Drive, MSC 6612
Bethesda, MD 20892-6612
(866) 284-4107 or (301) 496-5717
Web site: http://www3.niaid.nih.gov/topics/BiodefenseRelated
Information about chemical threats and countermeasures is
 available at the institute's Web site.

U.S. Department of Homeland Security
Washington, DC 20528
(202) 282-8000
Web site: http://www.dhs.gov
This is the federal department in overall charge of the war
 against terrorism.

Web Sites

Due to the changing nature of Internet links, Rosen Publishing
has developed an online list of Web sites related to the subject
of this book. This site is updated regularly. Please use this link
to access the list:

http://www.rosenlinks.com/sas/cbw

FOR FURTHER READING

Baker, David. *Biological, Nuclear, and Chemical Weapons: Fighting Terrorism*. Vero Beach, FL: Rourke Publishing, 2006.

Broyles, Janell. *Chemical and Biological Weapons in a Post-9/11 World* (The Library of Weapons of Mass Destruction). New York, NY: Rosen Publishing Group, 2004.

Gay, Kathlyn. *Silent Death: The Threat of Chemical and Biological Terrorism*. Brookfield, CT: Twenty-First Century Books, 2001.

Gibbs, Lynne, and Honor Head. *Mega Book of Weapons and Warfare: Discover the Most Amazing Weapons on Earth* (Mega Book Series). London, England: Chrysalis Children's Books, 2003.

Herbst, Judith. *The History of Weapons* (Major Inventions Through History). Brookfield, CT, Twenty-First Century Books, 2005.

Kerrigan, Michael. *Biological and Germ Warfare Protection* (Rescue and Prevention: Defending Our Nation). Broomall, PA: Mason Crest Publishers, 2003.

Levine, Herbert M. *Chemical & Biological Weapons in Our Times*. Danbury, CT: Franklin Watts, 2000.

Phillips, Tracy A. *Weapons of Mass Destruction: The Threat of Chemical, Biological, and Nuclear Weapons* (Issues in Focus Today). Berkeley Heights, NJ: Enslow Publishers, 2007.

BIBLIOGRAPHY

Associated Press. "Researchers Create Human Ricin Vaccine."
  January 31, 2006. Retrieved March 14, 2008 (http://www.
  nytimes.com/2006/01/31/politics/31ricin.html?_r=1&
  oref=slogin).

Associated Press. "Texas Student Finds Poison in Coin Roll."
  February 26, 2006. Retrieved March 14, 2008 (http://www.
  nytimes.com/2006/02/26/national/26ricin.html?_r=1&
  oref=slogin).

CNN.com. "Frist: Ricin Confirmed, But No Illness Reported."
  February 4, 2004. Retrieved March 14, 2008 (http://www.
  cnn.com/2004/US/02/03/senate.hazardous/index.html).

Dickey, Christopher. "T Is for Terror." MSNBC. *Newsweek* Web
  Exclusive, July 9, 2003. Retrieved March 14, 2008 (http://
  www.msnbc.msn.com/id/3070093).

Federation of American Scientists. "Anthrax Fact Sheet."
  Retrieved March 14, 2008 (http://www.fas.org/programs/ssp/
  bio/factsheets/H1N1factsheet.html).

Federation of American Scientists. "Botulinum Toxin Fact
  Sheet." Retrieved March 14, 2008 (http://www.fas.org/
  programs/ssp/bio/factsheets/botulinumfactsheet.html).

Federation of American Scientists. "Ebola Fact Sheet."
  Retrieved March 14, 2008 (http://www.fas.org/programs/ssp/
  bio/factsheets/ebolafactsheet.html).

Federation of American Scientists. "1918 Influenza A (H1N1)
  Fact Sheet." Retrieved March 14, 2008 (http://www.fas.org/
  programs/ssp/bio/factsheets/anthraxfactsheet.html).

Federation of American Scientists. "Ricin Fact Sheet." Retrieved
  March 14, 2008 (http://www.fas.org/programs/ssp/bio/
  factsheets/ricinfactsheet.html).

Federation of American Scientists. "Salmonella Fact Sheet." Retrieved March 14, 2008 (http://www.fas.org/programs/ssp/bio/factsheets/salmonellafactsheet.html).

Federation of American Scientists. "Sarin Fact Sheet." Retrieved March 14, 2008 (http://www.fas.org/programs/ssp/bio/factsheets/sarinfactsheet.html).

Friess, Steve. "Vials of Ricin Are Found in Las Vegas Hotel; Man Is Hospitalized." *New York Times*, March 1, 2008. Retrieved March 14, 2008 (http://www.nytimes.com/2008/03/01/us/01ricin.html).

Horowitz, Leonard. *Emerging Viruses: AIDS and Ebola—Nature, Accident or Genocide?* Rockport, MA: Tetrahedron, Inc., 1996.

Laqueur, Walter. *The New Terrorism: Fanaticism and the Arms of Mass Destruction.* New York, NY: Oxford University Press, 1999.

Lesser, Ian O., Bruce Hoffman, John Arquilla, David Ronfeldt, Michele Zanini, and Brian Michael Jenkins. *Countering the New Terrorism.* Santa Monica, CA: RAND Corporation, RAND Project AIR FORCE, 1999.

Mayor, Adrienne. *Greek Fire, Poison Arrows & Scorpion Bombs: Biological and Chemical Warfare in the Ancient World.* Woodstock, NY: Overlook Duckworth, 2003.

Packer, Adrienne. "Las Vegas Motel: Man Indicted on Ricin, Firearm Charges." *Las Vegas Review-Journal*, April 23, 2008. Retrieved April 23, 2008 (http://www.lvrj.com/news/18037054.html).

Public Broadcasting Service. "The Most Dangerous Woman in America." Documentary. Aired August 21, 2007. Retrieved March 14, 2008 (http://www.pbs.org/wgbh/nova/typhoid).

Simon, Jeffrey D. *The Terrorist Trap.* Bloomington and Indianapolis, IN: Indiana University Press, 2001.

Stern, Jessica. *Terror in the Name of God: Why Religious Militants Kill.* New York, NY: Ecco, 2003.

Tucker, Jonathan B. *War of Nerves: Chemical Warfare from World War I to Al-Qaeda.* New York, NY: Pantheon Books, 2006.

INDEX

About the Author

Daniel E. Harmon is the author of more than sixty books and a veteran periodicals editor and writer whose articles have appeared in many national and regional magazines and newspapers. *Careers in Explosives and Arson Investigation*, his book for Rosen Central's Careers in Forensics series, was published in 2008. His other educational books include volumes on the FBI, the Environmental Protection Agency, and the U.S. armed forces. He lives in Spartanburg, South Carolina.

Photo Credits